Carving Horse Portraits

in Relief

by Kurt Koch

Fox
Chapel Publishing Co. Inc.

1970 Broad Street • East Petersburg, PA 17520 • www.foxchapelpublishing.com

Publisher	Alan Giagnocavo
Project Editor	Ayleen Stellhorn
Desktop Specialist	Linda L. Eberly, Eberly Designs Inc.
Cover Design	Keren Holl

ISBN # 1–56523–180–5

To order your copy of this book,
please send check or money order
for the cover price plus $3.00 shipping to:
Fox Books
1970 Broad Street
East Petersburg, PA 17520

Or visit us on the web at
www.foxchapelpublishing.com

Printed in China

Table of Contents

Getting Started 1
   Using Basswood 1
   Carving Tools & Their Edges 2
   Reference Material 3

Step-By-Step 5
   Outline 5
   First Level 7
   Second Level 10
   Next Levels 12
   Base Level 14
   Features 18
   Backcutting 36
   Carving Hair 38
   Final Details 41

Demonstration Time Lapse 48

Reference Photos 51

Patterns 59

Gouge and Chisel Chart 67

CHAPTER ONE

Getting Started

Relief carving is the art of carving a subject so that it appears to be coming out of the wood. The subject is usually somewhat compressed. However, in high relief carving, such as shown in this book, the subject has more depth.

I am presenting a carving of a horse's head in high relief as a demonstration piece. The work is shown in progress, in a step-by-step fashion, to make it easier for the reader to follow. The individual steps are presented in a logical sequence with each step numbered. A picture of a mallet is shown where its use is suggested or recommended for that step.

All identifications for carving chisels and gouges are for straight-shafted tools. Cases where other specialty tools are used—such as curved, bent or spoon—will be identified separately. Proceed to work as far as possible with your own tools. Within small limits, you can replace the recommended tools with tools that you have on hand.

Using Basswood

Although basswood is a good carving wood, it is a relatively "dead" wood. What I mean is that its appearance does not show coloring or the annual growth and grain patterns that you would expect to find on harder woods like oak, ash, elm and cherry.

However, basswood is a very good wood for carving—especially so for relief carving. It takes very fine details very well. The colors and grains of the other woods mentioned earlier may distract or even detract from the view and details of a finely carved piece. You can be the world's greatest artistic carver, but if you choose a very colorful and well-patterned wood to show off your fine carving skills, you may find yourself in competition with Mother Nature herself. And as is her right, she may make your carving look second best to her own creation!

Two examples of extraordinarily heavy and long gouges. On the right, a Tirolean gouge; on the left a Swiss gouge.

Selection of the right wood for the sculpture you intend to carve is very important. Study your choice of wood and compare it to the subject matter and your skill level. The wood should match and complement your carving skills to maximize the beauty within the wood and highlight your finished piece. Be at one, as best as you can, with Mother Nature.

If you choose basswood for this piece, the relatively plain but textured background that is left by using a slightly curved chisel or gouge will not be in competition with your carving and will help demonstrate your skills.

Take care to fix the block on a solid table and use good quality clamps to avoid movement and vibration, especially when using the mallet during the roughing of the sculpture.

Do not place the block directly flat on a table or work surface. Add some small pieces of wood (all the same thickness) between the block and the table or work surface. This will allow for air circulation so the wood can breath. If this is not done, there is a danger that the block could warp or twist.

Carving Tools & Their Edges

Woodcarving tools can have, independent of their edge forms, different shaft shapes. This makes sense to make it possible to reach places not easily accessible with a straight-shafted tool. These tools with specially shaped shafts are fun to have, but are really only necessary in certain situations. As a general rule, most of the carving work in this book can be done with straight-shafted tools.

The straight-shafted tools are easiest to work with owing to the normal human hand and forearm anatomy. The starting angle for a cut is practically an extension of the main axis of your forearm and permits a large free movement of the hand. This is almost with-

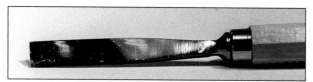

A straight chisel with a straight shaft and a straight edge (#1, 10 mm).

An example of a back-bent gouge.

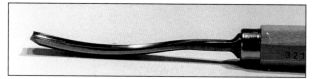

An example of a long bent tool (#8, 10mm).

Two examples of spoons. The edges are deeply concave.

out restriction compared to working with a shaped or "bent" tool shaft.

Derivation from the center of the shaft axis, such as found in curved shafts, makes it difficult for the carver to control the cut. Severe derivation, such as that found in the shafts of backbent and spoon chisels, make it extremely difficult, if not impossible to use a mallet. However, the difficulty in accessing the hard-to-reach areas of some carvings does require the use of these specially shaped tools. This is often the case with some ornamental and decorative carving where severe backcutting and undercutting around awkward shapes is required.

Fortunately for most carvers, the straight-shafted tools prove to be adequate for most of their work. It is an error for a beginner to assume that he needs some of these specially shaped tools in the early stages of learning woodcarving. Better that he equip himself with a good selection of straight-shafted tools and buy any specialty tools only as and when it is necessary. Once you have the knowledge and skills to try the more complicated pieces, then you will find out for yourself which of these special tools will be necessary or indispensable for your carving tool kit.

There are some carving tools that are really indispensable for every carver, for the professional as well as the beginner or hobbyist. These are the tools you will always need for the rest of your carving life. Many of these tools are used in this demonstration. They are listed on the following page.

Reference Material

I suggest that you collect as much reference material as possible before you begin a carving. I have included a number of reference photographs of live horses in the back of this book. It is my hope that you will use these photos to learn more about the muscle

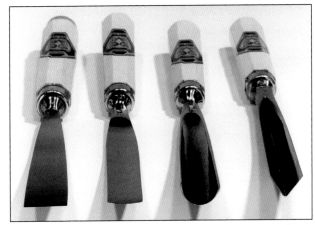

Examples of straight gouges. From left to right: Straight gouge (#1, 20 mm), flat gouge (#65, 20 mm), deeply fluted gouge (#10, 20 mm), and a v-tool (#41, 12 mm).

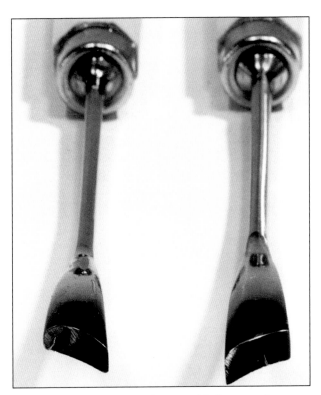

These bent-shaft gouges (above and below) are for special situations. The shaft is bent and the edge form slightly concave. One is diagonally ground to the left; the other to the right.

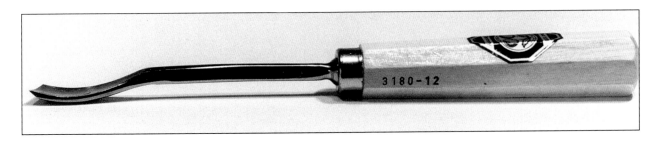

structure of your subject and that you will use them for inspiration for your next high relief carving project.

Tool Choice

The following tools are used throughout the demonstration. This list is for your information only. You may find that you can carve the horse in the demonstration without purchasing all these tools.

#1, 10 mm
#1, 20 mm
#3, 12 mm
#3, 25 mm
#4, 12 mm
#5, 14 mm
#5, 25 mm
#5, 30 mm
#6, 10 mm
#6, 14 mm
#6, 30 mm
#7, 20 mm
#8, 4 mm
#8, 8 mm
#8, 16 mm
#9, 6 mm
#9, 12 mm
#10, 2 mm
#10, 4 mm
#11, 1 mm
#11, 2 mm
#11, 4 mm
#39, 4 mm
#41, 12 mm
#65, 4 mm
#65, 16 mm
#65, 20 mm
#65, 25 mm
#65, 35 mm
#73, 10 mm

1 Copy the pattern of the horse's head to a well-seasoned block of wood. Pay close attention to placing the pattern in the center of the block. This block of wood measures approximately 10 inches wide, 13 3/8 inches high and 3 5/8 inches wide (25 by 33 by 9 centimeters).

2 Allow approximately one third of the block's thickness for the base, or background, of the sculpture. Mark that area off with a solid line. Evenly divide the remaining two-thirds space into six sections. Mark these areas with dashed lines.

3 The block of wood is now ready to cut. Notice how the horse's head is evenly centered on the block and how the lines on the side are clearly indicated. The horse's mane and neck will extend off the side of the block.

4 Using a large, slightly curved tool, mark in a line approximately 1/8 inch (2 mm) outside the pattern lines. Hold the tool at a slight angle so that the cut is made away from the horse's head. I recommend a #3, 25 mm gouge for this first step.

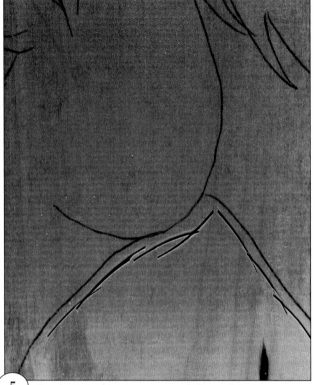

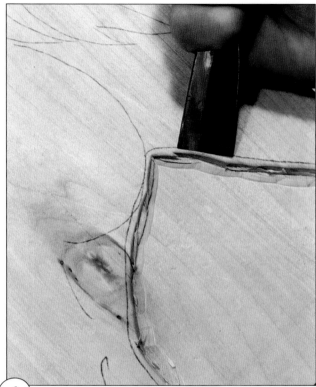

5 Continue making cuts around the entire outer pattern line. The cuts can overlap as this is only the start of the "roughing out" process. These cuts will form a border around the original pattern.

6 Still using the #3, 25 mm tool, deepen the outline cut to the depth of the first layer.

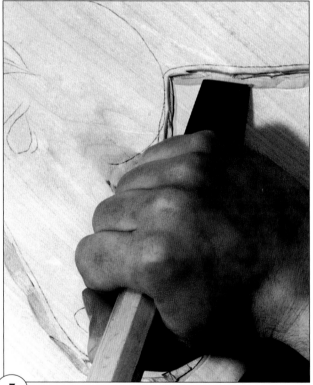

8 Holding the tool at a 45-degree angle, cut down to the deepest part of the border. Make an outline cut, then a longer cut from the outside line to the depth of the first cut. Repeat until you have reached the required depth. These cuts will give you a guideline for all similar work.

7 Make the cuts as uniformly deep as possible.

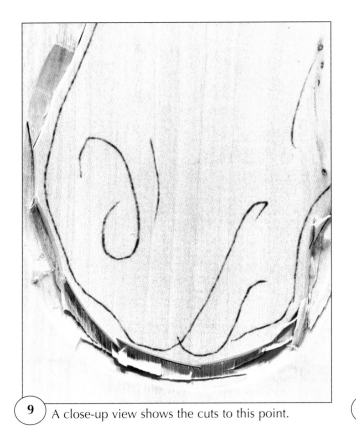

9 A close-up view shows the cuts to this point.

10 The entire horse portrait is outlined.

First Level

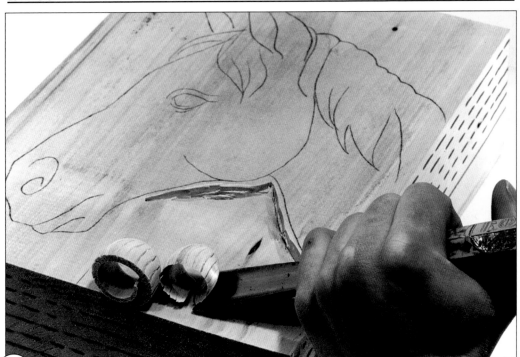

11 The best cutting direction for this step is across the grain. Use a larger gouge—either a #5, 30 mm or a #5, 25 mm.

12 The edges of the tool should not completely disappear from view into the wood. One side of the tool's edge should always be visible. This will help to show your progress and aid you in planning your next cut.

13 Try to maintain a consistent size and thickness to the shavings that you remove from the block.

14 The same shavings are seen here from a different angle. Notice how I have cut about halfway down to the dashed line that marks the depth of the first level.

15 Continue to make cuts across the grain to remove wood down to the first level of the background. These cuts are even with the dashed line for the first level.

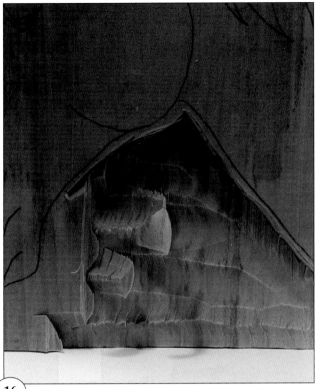

16 A look at the cuts from above shows how the cuts are overlapped as wood is removed.

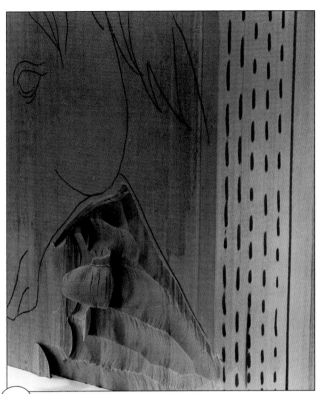

17 Viewing the cuts from the side, you can see how the cuts end abruptly at the outlines made in Step 10.

18 Continue to remove wood from the background down to the first level. Work across the grain. Start from the outside of the block and cut in to the outline of the horse. Hold the tool at a low angle.

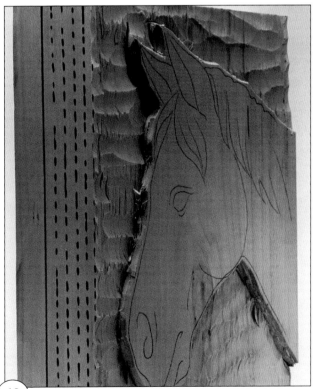

19 Shavings from these cuts should fall free as your cuts reach the outline. This is due to the cuts shown in Step 10.

20 Any shavings that do not fall free and are still attached at the end of a cut should be cut free. Avoid the temptation to tear away or break off a shaving—even those with very little connection to the wood. Tearing away or breaking off shavings is a bad habit and can damage a carving.

21 Once the background of the entire first level is removed, check the piece from all angles. Make sure that this first level is even all the way around the horse. If you marked the dashed lines correctly, this should not be an issue. If it is, check your dashed lines and correct them as necessary.

Second Level

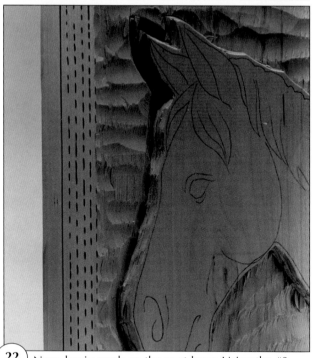

22 Now, begin work on the next layer. Using the #3, 25 mm or a #5, 30 mm gouge, make a new "notch" down to the second level of the background.

23 Continue this notch all the way around the entire outline of the horse's head.

Carving Horse Portraits in Relief

24 A close-up photograph of the ear area shows the new notch that was cut down to the depth of the second level.

25 An extreme close-up from a different angle shows the cuts from the first and second rounds of notches. Notice how these cuts are still about 1/8 inch (2 mm) from the pattern outline.

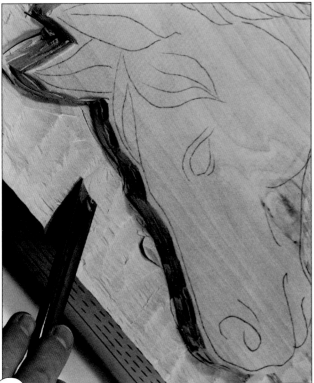

26 Working again across the grain, remove wood from the background down to the dashed line that marks the second level. Use the #5, 30 mm gouge for this step.

27 Looking at the project from above, you can see that the background of the second level has been removed from the forehead to just before the mouth.

28 A view from the side shows the same cuts. Again, the shavings should fall free from the block as your tool reaches the notches you cut in Step 23.

29 If the depth of the second level is even all the way around the horse's head, create notches for the third level and move on to removing wood to the next depth.

30 A view from the side shows how these cuts are now reaching the depth of the third level.

31 Work continues down to the fourth level. Again, notice how 1/8 inch of wood is left between the cuts and the pattern outline.

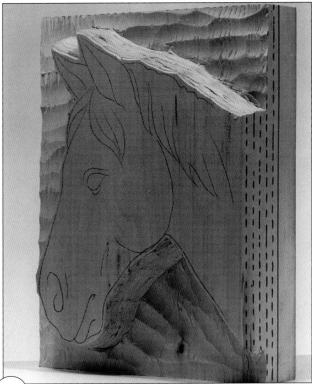

32 A check of the work at this point shows that the fourth level is even all the way around. Notice how there are only two sections left above and below the horse's neck.

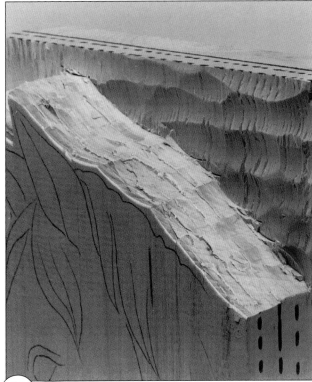

33 This close-up photograph shows the wood removal to this point. By studying the edge of the horse's mane, it is apparent that the wood has been removed in levels. Only two more levels to go.

Base Level

34 All the background wood has been removed. A block under the horse's nose helps the now-top-heavy block to stand.

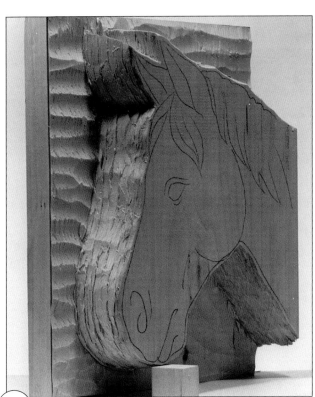

35 A view from the side shows how the wood is removed down to the solid line that marks the final depth of the background.

36 A closer view shows the rough edges of each of the levels as they were notched. All of these notches were cut at a slight angle and about 1/8 inch away from the profile of the horse's head. This gives a nice margin of safety for the final shaping.

37 A view from the neck shows the original dashed lines indicating the six levels of wood that were removed to reach this final depth.

Clean-Up

38 Now the clean up begins. Using a #1, 20 mm chisel, start at the flat area of the horse's nose and make perpendicular cuts from the highest level of the carving to the deepest level of the background.

39 Follow the original pattern line as closely as possible. The cleaner your cuts are at this stage, the easier it will be to continue the project.

40 You may need to use several different gouges to complete the outline. Choose a tool that most closely matches the shape of the area that you are cutting. I used the following tools on this step: a #1, 20 mm; a #65, 25 mm; a #8, 08mm; and a #41, 12mm.

41 A view looking across the work from the horse's neck shows the perpendicular cuts made in these areas.

42 A close up of the ears shows the perpendicular cuts here.

43 Work continues to make the perpendicular cuts around the outline of the horse's head.

44 A close-up view of this same area gives you a good look at the cuts.

45 With the piece on its back, you will notice how deep this relief carving will be. This depth is typical for a "high relief" carving.

46 A final round of clean-up work is done with a #65, 35 mm gouge and a #2, 4 mm gouge where the perpendicular cuts meet the background.

47 Continue to clean up the area where the neck meets the background.

48 Clean up continues around the entire outline of the horse's head.

49 A view from the front shows the clean-up work that was done on this section

50 A view from the back shows the clean-up work that was done on this section.

51 A final view from the top shows the clean-up work that was done here.

52 Using a red marker, highlight the area where wood will be removed to form the base of the ear.

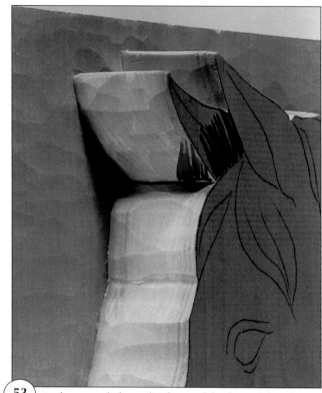

53 A photograph from the front of the horse's head shows how this mark continues around to the front of the ear.

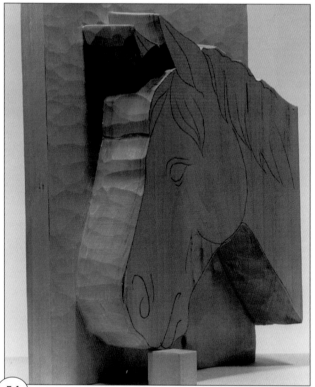

54 Using a #3, 25 mm gouge and a #1, 10 mm chisel, remove the marked wood.

55 A close-up photograph shows how the cuts should look at this point.

Mane

56 Mark the area under the mane with a red marker. This will be the next area to be removed.

57 Notice how the marks extend onto the side of the horse's neck. The deepest part of the cut should reach the second level of the background.

58 Using a #1, 10 mm chisel and a #3, 25 mm gouge, outline the mane.

59 A close up of the mane shows the cuts in this area.

Forelock

60 Notice how a section of the mane extends between the horse's ears to lie just above the eye. This tuft of hair is referred to as the forelock. Outline this area with a red marker. This section will be relieved next.

61 Using a #3, 25 mm gouge, a #73, 10 mm gouge and a #4, 12mm gouge, remove the wood around this section of the mane.

62 Notice how the cuts that outline this section are only as deep as the cuts that outline the mane. They are not as deep as the cuts made to establish the base of the right ear.

63 Mark the right ear and the top of the mane for the next cuts.

64 Notice how the marks for the mane and the ear extend over the top and side of the horse's head.

65 Another photo from the top of the horse's head shows the extent of the wood that will be removed.

66 Using a #5, 25 mm gouges and a #3, 12mm gouge, rough in the mane and the right ear.

67 Notice how the right ear has been lowered according to the marks.

68 Mark the wood that will be removed from the neck area below the mane. Note how the marks extend into the third level.

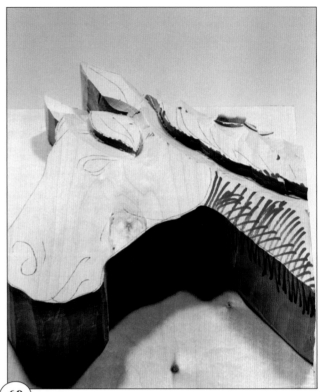

69 A photo from this angle shows how the marks extend to the bottom of the neck.

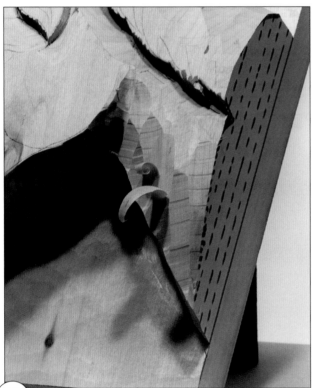

70 Using a #5, 25 mm gouge and a #4, 12 mm gouge, remove the wood from the neck area below the mane. Notice how the wood is removed only up to the lower jaw area of the horse's head.

71 A view looking across the carving from the horse's neck shows how deeply these cuts have been made.

72) Mark the wood to be removed from the front of the horse's head.

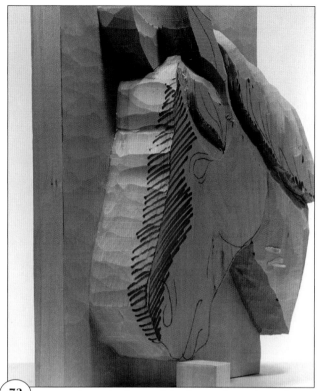

73) A view from the front of the horse shows how the marks extend onto the front of the carving.

74) Remove the wood indicated by the red lines in the previous step with a #5, 25 mm gouge and a #4, 12 mm gouge.

75) A slightly different view shows the depth of the wood removed.

Forelock

76 Mark the wood to be removed from the sections of the mane that extend between the horse's ears.

77 Notice that there are two sections of the forelock on this particular sculpture: one that falls on the front of the face above the eye, and one that falls back toward the right ear.

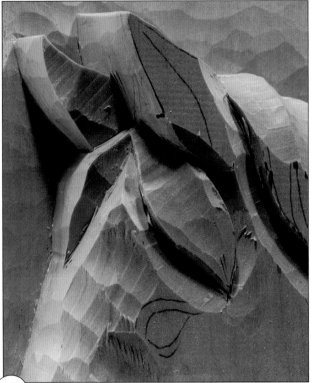

78 Using a #5, 25 mm gouge and a #73, 10 mm gouge, remove the wood from the forelocks.

79 A front view of the cuts shows how this area should look at this point.

Lower Jaw

80 Mark the wood to be removed from the mouth and lower jaw of the horse's head.

81 A view from a different angle shows how the marks extend around to the underside and muzzle of this area.

82 Remove the wood as indicated in the previous photograph with a #5, 25 mm gouge and a #73, 10 mm gouge.

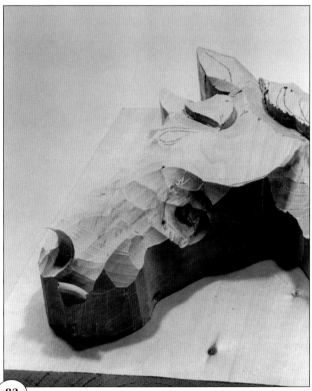

83 A view from below shows the wood that has been removed. Note the before-unnoticed knot of wood that indicates where a branch once grew out of the tree. I chose to work the knot into the finished carving, rather than scrap the entire piece.

84 Mark the wood to be removed from the upper part of the lower jaw. Study reference materials if you are not familiar with the look of a strong jaw on a horse.

85 A view from the underside of the horse's head shows how deep the cuts will go in this area.

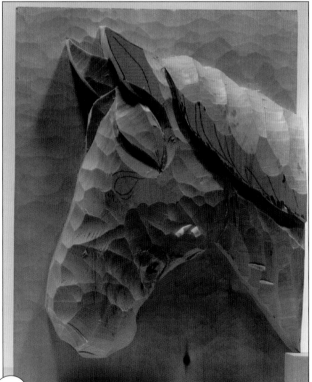

86 Remove the wood from the jaw. Note how all the areas blend together even though the depths of the areas may be slightly different.

87 A photograph from this angle shows the area where the neck meets the jaw. Also notice the depths of the facial cuts as compared to those of the mane and forelock.

88 Mark the wood to be removed around the eye. The area under the eye is marked more heavily because additional wood will be removed from that area.

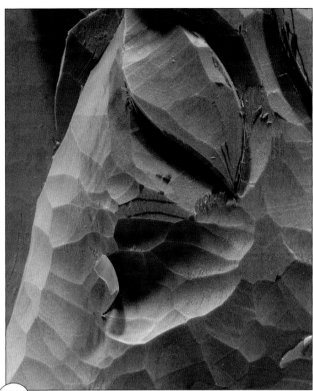

89 Using a #4, 12 mm gouge, a #5, 14 mm gouge and a #8, 16 mm gouge, remove the wood from around the eye.

90 A view from the front of the horse shows the depth of the cuts around the eye. This rough carving gives the eye a definite position in the face.

91 A photograph taken from this angle shows the depth of the cut underneath the eye. Note how deep the cut is when compared to the rough cuts around the forelock.

92 Mark the wood to be removed from the left ear and from area where the mane overlaps the neck.

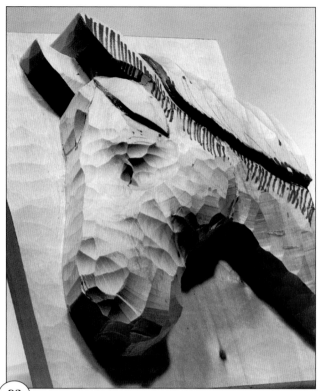

93 A view from this angle shows how the marks wrap to the front of the ear.

94 Remove the wood from the front of the left ear and from the neck where the mane overlays the neck. Use several gouges for this step: #5, 14 mm; #4, 12mm; #8, 16 mm; and #5, 25 mm.

95 Here you can see the amount of wood removed from both areas.

Mane

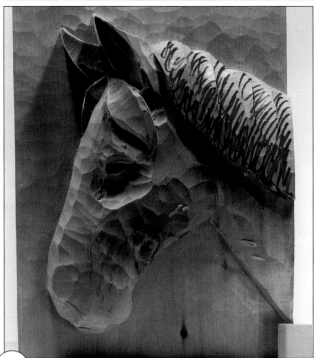

96 Mark in the basic form of the mane. Notice how the lines from the marker roughly show how the hair will fall across the horse's neck.

97 A view from this angle shows that wood will not be removed from the very top of the mane. Notice also that no wood will be removed from the edge of the carving where the depth marks are indicated.

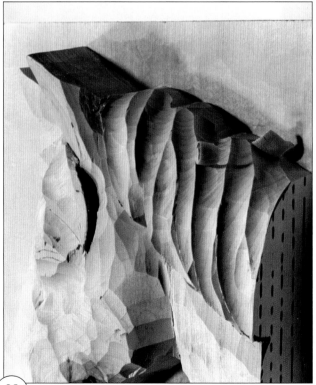

98 Remove the wood from the mane in several continuous bottom-to-top sweeps. Use several gouges for this step: #5, 14 mm; #4, 12 mm; #8, 16 mm; and #5, 25 mm.

99 Notice how the "sweeps" of the mane are starting to take shape.

100 Step back and take a look at the horse's face at this point. The ears, the mane and the shape of the face have been roughed in.

101 Mark the wood to be removed from the neck. This will be a slight undercutting of the neck (under the mane) up onto the back of the left ear.

102 Remove the wood with a series of gouges: a #5, 14 mm; a #65, 16 mm; a #73, 10 mm; a #8, 16 mm; and a #5, 25 mm. Notice how the left ear is clearly situated in front of the mane.

Ear/Forelock ■■■■■

103 Mark the wood to be removed from the inside of the left ear and from the top of the forelock.

104 Remove the wood from these areas with a #6, 14 mm gouge; a #73, 10 mm gouge; a #8, 4 mm gouge; and a #11, 04 mm gouge.

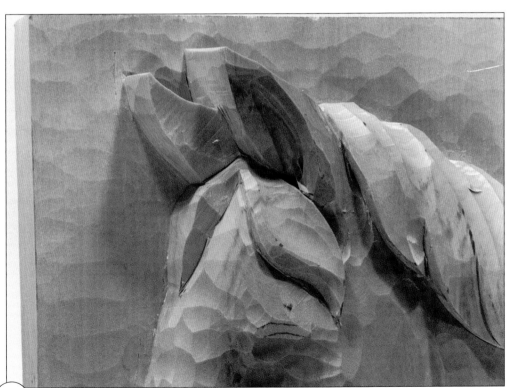

105 Note how the wood has been removed quite deeply from the inside of the left ear and only slightly from the top of the forelock.

106 Mark the wood to be removed from the ears and the back section of the forelock.

107 A view from the front shows the marks for the wood that will be removed from the back of the left ear.

108 Remove the wood with a #73, 10 mm gouge, a #5, 14 mm gouge, and a #2, 4 mm gouge Notice how much life this backcutting adds to these elements.

109 Mark the area around the eye for the final rough carving and positioning of the eye.

110 Remove the wood with a #9, 12 mm gouge and a #8, 8 mm gouge. A photograph taken from the front of the piece shows the positioning of the eye in relation to the front of the face.

111 Notice how the eye is not flat on the face. It angles down into the mound of the eye area.

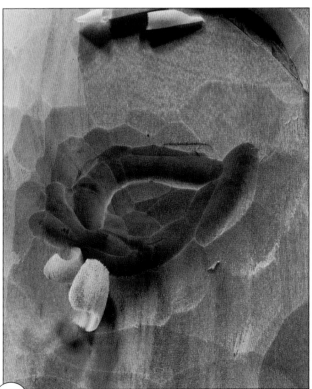

112 A close up of the eye shows the gouge marks that outline the final shape of the eye.

Mouth/Nose

113 Mark the wood to be removed from the mouth and lower jaw.

114 A view from under the jaw shows how these marks wrap around to the underside of the mouth.

115 Use a #5, 25 mm; a #65, 16 mm; and a #7, 20 mm to removed the wood from the mouth and the lower jaw.

116 Notice the appearance of a knot on the side of the horse's jaw. Unexpected surprises are part of working with wood. Such surprises should not detract from the final piece and should serve to emphasize that the carving is a natural work of art!

117 Mark the wood to be removed from the nose and the mouth.

118 Remove the wood with a series of gouges: a #8, 8 mm; a #5, 25 mm; a #3, 12 mm; a #6, 10 mm; and a #7, 20 mm.

119 A close-up photograph of the nose and mouth shows the rough-carved nostril and mouth.

120 A view from the top shows the amount of wood that was removed from the nose and the placement of the nostril.

Backcutting

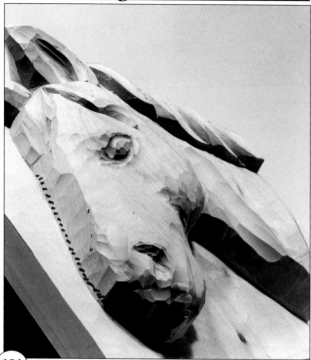

121 Mark the area where the horse's head meets the background in the areas shown. Backcutting the head will help the carving to stand out from the background.

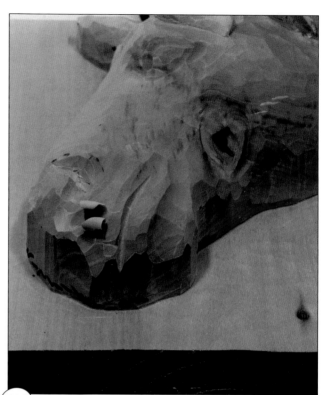

122 The marks for the area to be backcut extend around the nose and under the jaw.

123 Using a #3, 12 mm gouge; a #73, 10 mm gouge; and a #2, 4 mm gouge, remove the small amount of wood to backcut where the horse's head meets the background.

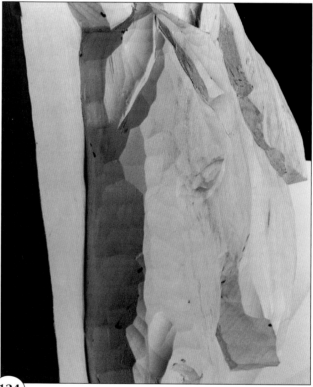

124 A view from the front shows a different angle. Notice how shadows are created in the backcut areas. Though this backcutting may not be seen when the finished piece is displayed, care should be taken to execute these cuts correctly.

Ears

125 Mark the wood to be removed from both ears.

126 A view from above shows how the marks wrap around to the tops of both ears.

127 Use a #3, 12 mm gouge; a #65, 20 mm gouge; a #73, 10 mm gouge; and a #2, 8 mm gouge to shape the ears.

128 A close-up view shows the final rough carving and positioning of the ears.

129 A photograph taken from the front of the horse shows how the left ear is now completely free of the background.

Carving Horse Portraits in Relief

Carving Hair

Before we continue with the demonstration, let me offer some additional words on the carving of hair.

Don't ever use the V-tool exclusively to carve hair. The straight profiles of the tool make it more difficult to get a smooth, controlled, curving cut. Hair carved only with a V-tool appears 'slicked back,' lifeless and devoid of movement—as though you used hair cream on your subject.

The First Cuts

For the first, basic cuts, I recommend gouges up to 6 mm with a cutting profile between 6 and 9. These tools allow a sweeping movement and cuts in three dimensions, the same dimensions as real hair. You can move your cuts forward and to the side, making the cuts shallower or deeper into the wood as you cut. You should practice this technique before you approach a final piece. Strive to establish a feel for the basic cuts that will create lifelike hair.

The basic cuts, as well as the following cuts, should not be parallel, or side by side. Each cut can be and should be varied in depth, in width or in length. The preliminary cuts can be wider, deeper and longer than the final cuts. A new cut should not have the same starting point as the previous cut.

With the first basic cuts you will set the form of the hair and its position. These basic cuts will determine the final form of the hair. If done carefully and correctly, the final appearance of the hair will be natural looking; if not, it will look totally false. Make these basic cuts with profiles 8 to 11.

The Second Cuts

Into these basic cuts, make a second series of cuts for more detail. Use smaller gouges, 2 to 3 mm wide. Try not to make the cuts parallel or identical in depth.

Strive to bring movement to the hair. You can start a new cut at almost any place and make a short trace at the end of a cut. You can make the cut longer but, as already mentioned, not parallel to existing cuts. You can also swing a new cut into an existing cut.

You can also create a new cut from one of the basic cuts, but please don't do this in isolation without some final form in mind. These second cuts should help to create the illusion of natural hair. Also try to avoid re-cutting existing cuts with smaller gouges or going over existing cuts.

The Third Cuts

For the third and final series of cuts, I suggest you select a small and deeply fluted tool: a #11, 2 mm or a #47, 1 mm tool is ideal. These tools should not be used for long cuts in hair, but for fine and small cuts. As a general rule, the length of the cuts made with these tools should be about three times the width of the original basic cuts.

With these small and deeply fluted gouges you have more freedom of movement to follow and make small cuts within existing larger cuts. You could use a very small 1 mm V-tool, but in general, you would have a problem making these same cuts with a V-tool. Another and perhaps easier option to a V-tool is to make additional cuts into the basic cuts with a chip carving knife or a small carving knife.

Mane

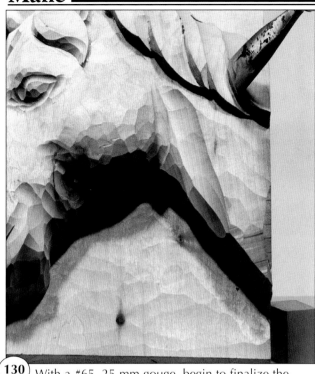

130 With a #65, 25 mm gouge, begin to finalize the mane.

131 Continue to use the #65, 25 mm gouge to separate the sections of the mane.

132 A close-up shot of the mane shows the definitions that are added to the bottom of the mane.

133 Another view of the mane shows the depth and angles of the cuts made in Steps 130 and 131.

Forelock

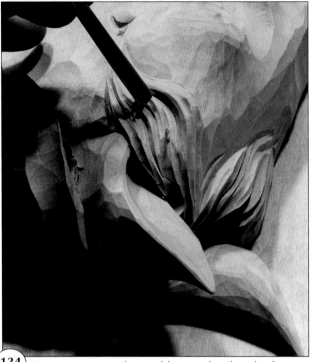

134 Now you are ready to add more detail to the forelocks. (See the sidebar on carving hair on page 38.) Use three different gouges shapes to create the hair. Start with a #8, 4 mm or a #9, 6 mm gouge. Both of these gouges have a gentle sweep.

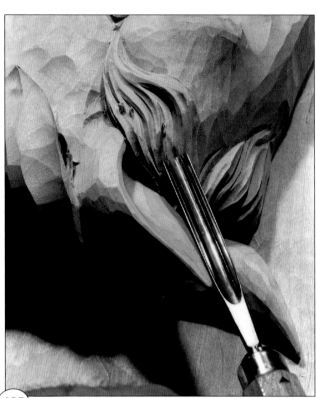

135 Add more concave cuts with a #11, 1 mm or a #10, 2 mm gouge. Both of these gouges are U-shaped.

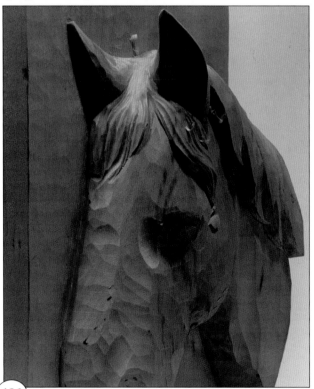

136 Finally, add some irregular cuts with a #39, 4 mm gouge. This gouge has a V shape.

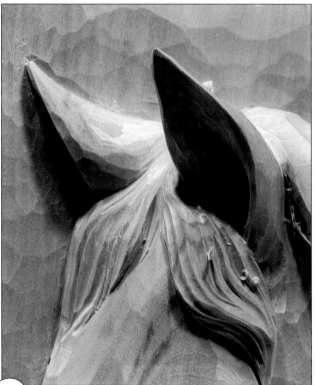

137 A close-up photograph of the forelocks shows the different textures of the hair. Note that all the hair sweeps in the same direction but does not necessarily follow the same path.

138 Try to develop a rhythmic motion when you make cuts for hair. Strive to make clean cuts so that the end result appears natural.

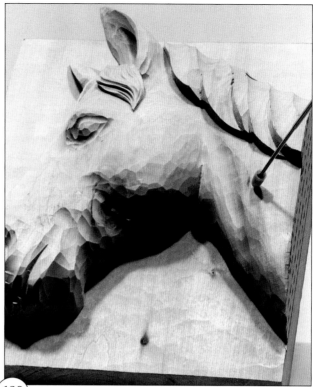

139 Smooth the surface of the neck with a #6, 10 mm gouge; a #65, 20 mm gouge; a #73, 10 mm gouge; and a #2, 18 mm gouge.

Final Details

140 Carve the details of the eye with a number of gouges: a #6, 10 mm; 1 # 73, 10 mm; a #8, 8 mm; a #8, 16 mm, a #11, 2 mm, a #10, 4 mm; a #9, 12 mm; a #65, 4 mm; and a #2, 4 mm.

141 Smooth the surface of the face with gouges. Carve in the typical vein formation found on the noses of most horses. (The vein is optional.)

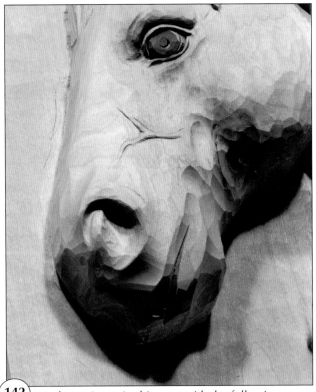

142 Work continues in this area with the following gouges: a #65, 4 mm; a #73, 10 mm; a #65, 20 mm; and a #2, 8 mm gouge.

143 Carve the details of the nostril and mouth.

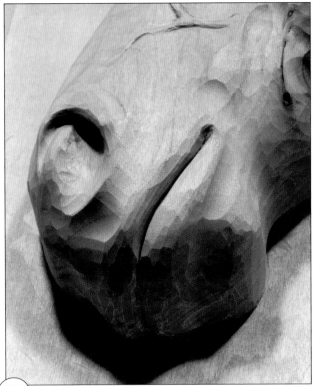

144 The following gouges and chisel are used in this area: a #1, 1 mm; a #6, 10 mm, a #10, 4 mm; a #65, 4 mm; a #11, 2 mm; a #73, 10 mm; a #8, 16 mm; a #8, 8 mm; a #9, 12 mm; and a #2, 18 mm.

145 Do the final carving of the mane with the following gouges: a #10, 4mm a #9, 6mm; a #10, 2 mm; a #8, 4 mm; a #39, 4 mm; and a #2, 8 mm.

146 A close-up photograph of the detailed mane shows the various cuts used to give it motion and make it look lifelike.

147 A view from the back of the horse shows the varying depths used in the cuts that detail the mane.

148 Notice how the hair of the mane and the hair of the forelocks have the same general characteristics.

The final presentation of the relief-carved horse. The finished piece can be stained. I recommend a 1:1 mix of a weak and medium walnut stain. Staining the wood twice will deepen the color.

Demonstration Time Lapse

A series of summary photos gives you a quick look at the basic steps of the previous demonstration. For more information, refer back to the step number listed under the photo.

Step 1: Transfer the pattern.

Step 2: Mark the levels.

Step 10: Outline.

Step 19: Remove Level 1.

Step 23: Outline next levels.

Step 35: Remove levels.

Step 49: Clean up.

Step 52: Mark the ear.

Step 55: Carve the ear.

Step 56: Mark the mane.

Step 58: Outline the mane.

Step 60: Mark the forelock.

Step 61: Outline the forelock.

Step 63:Mark the mane/ear.

Step 66: Rough in the mane.

Step 68: Mark the neck.

Step 70: Carve the neck.

Step 72: Mark the head.

Step 74: Carve the head.

Step 76: mark the ears/mane.

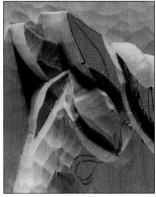
Step 78: Carve the ears/mane.

Step 80: Mark the mouth.

Step 82: Carve the mouth.

Step 84: Mark the jaw.

Step 86: Carve the jaw.

Step 88: Mark the eye.

Step 89: Carve the eye.

Step 92: Mark the mane edge.

Step 94: Carve the mane edge.

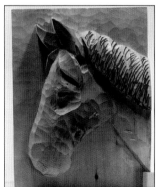
Step 96: Mark the mane.

Step 100: Carve the mane.

Step 107: Mark the ears.

Step 108: Carve the ears.

Step 110: Carve the eye.

Step 113: Mark the mouth.

Step 116: Carve the mouth.

Step 117: Mark the nose.

Step 119: Carve the nose.

Step 121: Mark backcuts.

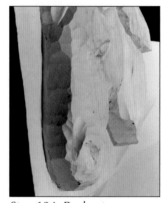

Step 124: Backcut.

Step 125: Mark the ears.

Step 129: Carve the ears.

Step 130: Section the mane.

Step 135: Detail the forelocks.

Step 143: Detail the eye/nose.

Step 147: Detail the mane.

Reference Photos

Reference Photos

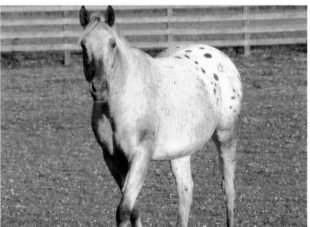

Pattern

Pattern

© Kurt Koch

Pattern

© Kurt Koch

Pattern

Pattern

© Kurt Koch

Gouge and Chisel Chart

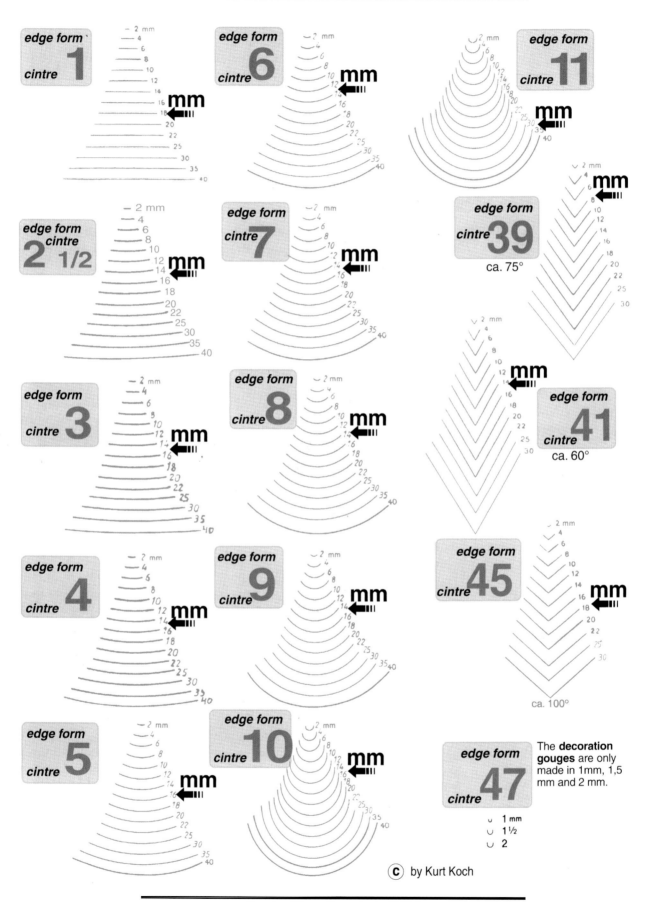

SUBSCRIBE TODAY!

DON'T MISS ANOTHER ISSUE OF SCROLL SAW WORKSHOP

☐ **ONE YEAR** Subscription

☐ $19.95 USA
☐ $22.50 Canada - US Funds Only
☐ $27.95 Int'l - US Funds Only

☐ **TWO YEAR** Subscription

☐ $39.90 USA
☐ $45.00 Canada - US Funds Only
☐ $55.90 Int'l - US Funds Only

Please allow 4-6 weeks for delivery

Four issues per year

☐ Bill Me ☐ Check/Money Order
☐ Visa, MC or Discover

Name on card _____

Exp. date _____ Telephone ( ) _____
cardnumber

[ ][ ][ ][ ][ ][ ][ ][ ][ ][ ][ ][ ][ ][ ][ ][ ]

Send To:

Name: _____
Address: _____
_____
City: _____
State/Prov.: _____
Zip: _____
Telephone: _____ Country: _____

VISA | MasterCard | DISCOVER NOVUS | CFBN

SCROLL SAW TOYS AND VEHICLES
A Complete Technique and Project Pattern Manual
By Stan Graves

FREE
with a two-year
paid subscription

Subscription order desk 888-840-8590

SUBSCRIBE TODAY!

DON'T MISS ANOTHER ISSUE OF WOOD CARVING ILLUSTRATED

☐ **ONE YEAR** Subscription

☐ $19.95 USA
☐ $22.50 Canada - US Funds Only
☐ $27.95 Int'l - US Funds Only

☐ **TWO YEAR** Subscription

☐ $39.90 USA
☐ $45.00 Canada - US Funds Only
☐ $55.90 Int'l - US Funds Only

Please allow 4-6 weeks for delivery

Four issues per year

☐ Bill Me ☐ Check/Money Order
☐ Visa, MC or Discover

Name on card _____

Exp. date _____ Telephone ( ) _____
cardnumber

[ ][ ][ ][ ][ ][ ][ ][ ][ ][ ][ ][ ][ ][ ][ ][ ]

Send To:

Name: _____
Address: _____
_____
City: _____
State/Prov.: _____
Zip: _____
Telephone: _____ Country: _____

VISA | MasterCard | DISCOVER NOVUS | CFBN

Power Carving MANUAL
How to Carve Wood - over 500+ color photos
A Special Edition from your friends at Wood Carving Illustrated Magazine
BIRD CARVING Step-by-Step
207 Bits & Burs for Carvers
Carving Gun Stocks
Sign Making

FREE
with a two-year
paid subscription

Subscription order desk: 888-506-6630

FREE BOOK CATALOG

YES! *I'd like a free catalog of your woodworking titles. Please place me on your mailing list and send me a copy right away.*

Previously purchased titles:
_____
_____

I'm particularly interested in: *(circle all that apply)*   General Woodworking   Woodcarving   Scroll Sawing   Cabinetmaking   Nature Drawing

Suggestion box: I think Fox Chapel should do a book about:
_____
_____

Bonus: Give us your email address to receive free updates.

Send to:
Name: _____ Email Address: _____
Address: _____ City: _____
State/Prov.: _____
Telephone: _____ Country: _____ Zip: _____

Visit us on the web at www.Foxchapelpublishing.com
or call us at 800-457-9112

AFB00

From:_____

City:_____
State/Prov.:_____
Country:_____Zip:_____

Scroll Saw
WorkShop
The How-To Magazine for Scrollers

1970 Broad St.
East Petersburg PA 17520   USA

From:_____

City:_____
State/Prov.:_____
Country:_____Zip:_____

Wood Carving
I L L U S T R A T E D

1970 Broad St.
East Petersburg PA 17520   USA

From:_____

City:_____
State/Prov.:_____
Country:_____Zip:_____

Fox
Chapel Publishing Co. Inc.

Free Catalog Offer
1970 Broad St.
East Petersburg PA 17520   USA